**Pet Projects**

# Handy
# HORSE
# Projects

*Lots of cool craft projects inside*

Isabel Thomas

raintree
a Capstone company — publishers for children

D0996396

Raintree is an imprint of Capstone Global Library Limited, a company incorporated in England and Wales having its registered office at 7 Pilgrim Street, London, EC4V 6LB – Registered company number: 6695582

www.raintree.co.uk
myorders@raintree.co.uk

Edited by Helen Cox Cannons and Holly Beaumont
Designed by Philippa Jenkins
Picture research by Tracy Cummins
Production by Helen McCreath
Originated by Capstone Global Library Ltd
Printed and bound in China

ISBN 978 1 406 29821 5
19 18 17 16 15
10 9 8 7 6 5 4 3 2 1

**British Library Cataloguing in Publication Data**
A full catalogue record for this book is available from the British Library.

**Acknowledgements**
We would like to thank the following for permission to reproduce photographs:
Shutterstock: Brooke Whatnall, Design Element, Eric Isselee, 1, Multiple Use, 29 Bottom, Design Element, Graeme Dawes, 11 Top, YanLev, Cover Bottom Left.

All other photography by Capstone Studio: Karon Dubke.

Every effort has been made to contact copyright holders of material reproduced in this book. Any omissions will be rectified in subsequent printings if notice is given to the publisher.

**Safety instructions for adult helper**
Some of the projects in this book involve steps that should only be carried out by an adult – these are indicated in the text. Always follow the instructions carefully.

# Contents

Look out for the hoof-print icons. These tell you how long each project will take.

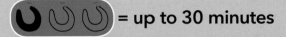 = up to 30 minutes

 = up to 1 hour

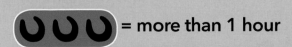 = more than 1 hour

# Hooked on horses

It's impossible to get enough of those big brown eyes and velvety noses. If you are lucky enough to ride or own a horse – or just love petting every pony you pass – you'll find some amazing ideas in this book.

- ✖ Make gifts for friends or relatives
- ✖ Decorate your bedroom with horse designs
- ✖ Create homemade treats and toys
- ✖ Throw a pony party!

At the back of the book you'll find a link to a web page packed with templates to use in the projects, and tips on how to use them to create designs of your own!

## Getting started

Before starting each project, read the instructions carefully and make sure you have everything you need. Find out if you will need an adult to help with any of the steps. If you are planning to recycle an object, or decorate walls, clothes or furniture, check that it's ok first.

Healthy horse biscuits
page 10

Pony pottery
page 20

Photo frames
page 9

## Working safely

Work in an area where you can make a mess, using newspaper to protect the table or floor. If you are using paint or glue, make sure you open the windows or work outside. Keep pets away while you are crafting. Never use paint or glue near a pet – the fumes can be dangerous for animals.

## Pet view

Look out for my top tips as you gallop through the book!

## Things... to keep in your craft kit

- Scissors, pens, pencils, paints, paintbrush, ruler, sticky tape and PVA glue.

- Scraps of pretty fabric, paper, card, newspapers and magazines.

- Boxes, jars and containers with interesting shapes (wash and dry food containers before storing them).

- Pretty found objects such as feathers, stones and buttons.

- Sewing materials such as needle and thread, wool, yarn, ribbons and trimmings.

5

# Upcycle!

You can recycle almost anything, from pony magazines to used horseshoes. Saddle up with these cheap and fun upcycling projects.

## File style

Découpage is a way of decorating with cut or torn paper. It's also a great way to recycle pretty pony wrapping paper that you can't bear to throw away. Follow these steps to turn a cereal box into stylish storage.

**1** Mark a diagonal line across the sides of a cereal box as shown. Cut along the lines to remove the top of the box.

**2** Cut or tear the magazines, cards or wrapping paper into pieces big enough to show off the pictures or patterns.

**3** Paint a small area of the cereal box with diluted PVA glue. Stick on pieces of the cut or torn paper, overlapping the edges.

### You will need:

- cereal box
- ruler and pencil
- scissors
- paintbrush
- old horse magazines, greetings cards or wrapping paper
- diluted PVA glue (3 parts glue to 1 part water)

**4** Repeat until you have covered the cereal box with pictures, and leave it to dry.

**5** To seal and protect your design, brush it with a coat of diluted PVA glue. Leave it to dry overnight before adding a second coat.

# 5 ways... to decorate with découpage

🎗 Look out for interesting containers in charity shops, and give them a stylish découpage makeover.

🎗 Cover a photo or mirror frame with horse and pony pictures.

🎗 Ask an adult to help you cut a horse shape in thick card (see page 31 for information on how to access templates online). Decorate using découpage to make a unique piece of wall art.

🎗 Use découpage to decorate a name plaque for your pony's stable door. Ask an adult to help you give it two coats of clear varnish to make it waterproof.

🎗 Brighten up a plastic or metal bin by covering it in découpage horses.

# Three ways to decorate with old horse shoes

There are lots of different ways to decorate with horseshoes. You can find used horseshoes at a farrier's yard, a scrapyard or an antiques centre. You can also make your own out of cardboard, using a template from the website (see page 31).

(see page 31)

 **TOP TIP**

Before you customize a used horseshoe, ask an adult to remove any nails using pliers. You can clean the shoe using a steel brush or wire wool. Add a coat of paint to stop it rusting.

## Hang a lucky horse shoe

Glue on beads or spell out the name of your favourite horse. Thread each end of a ribbon through two of the holes in the shoe, and hang the horseshoe on a door or cupboard handle.

Many people believe that horseshoes are lucky charms.

### Pet view

My shoes need refitting by a farrier every six to eight weeks. That's a lot of old shoes!

## Bedroom tack rack

Ask an adult to help you nail one or more horseshoes to a block of wood, leaving some nails sticking out at different lengths. Fix the block on to a wall, and hang bracelets and necklaces from the nails.

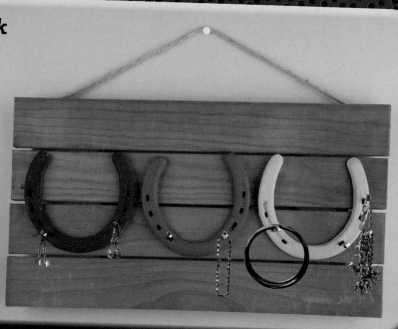

## In the frame

Paint a group of horseshoes in bright colours, and ask an adult to help you hang them together on a wall. Use them as a place to store important mail, or cut photos to fit and use them as quirky photo frames.

# Kitchen creations

Horses love yummy treats, and it's hard to say no when a velvety nose nuzzles into your hands. Get creative in the kitchen by baking these healthy treats!

## Healthy horse biscuits

Sugary snacks such as sugar lumps and peppermints can be bad for horses and ponies. Try offering these homemade horse biscuits instead.

**1** Grate the carrots, and mix them with the jar of unsweetened apple sauce, oatmeal and enough water to make a sticky dough.

**2** Roll the dough into balls and put them on a baking sheet. Ask an adult to bake them in an oven at 180°C (350°F) for 10 minutes.

**3** When the biscuits have cooled, cut them into small pieces and store in an airtight container.

### You will need:

- two carrots
- small jar of unsweetened apple sauce
- 128 g (4½ oz.) oatmeal
- water

# 5 books... every horse lover should read

Gallop down to your local library to track down these brilliant reads.

- *The Horses of Follyfoot* by Monica Dickens
- *Black Beauty* by Anna Sewell
- *A Horse For Angel* by Sarah Lean
- *The One-Dollar Horse* by Lauren St John
- *A Horse Called Hero* by Sam Angus

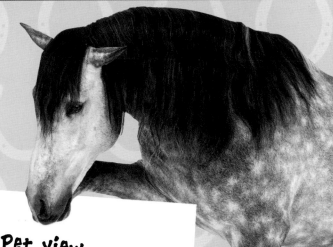

## Pet view

Feed me treats from a bucket rather than by hand. This will stop me developing bad habits! Some fresh fruits and vegetables make good treats, in small amounts, but others can make me sick. Ask your vet for a list.

# Fantastic fabric projects

Hunt down pretty horse fabrics in your local haberdashery or craft shop, and try these simple projects.

## Pendant key holder

This horseshoe key holder doubles as a pretty pendant. Use it to keep a house key, diary key or stable key close to your heart.

**1** Cut a horseshoe-shaped piece of felt, using the template from the website (see page 31). Then use another template to cut two identical bell-shaped felt pieces in a pretty, contrasting colour.

**2** Sew the pieces of felt together along the curved edges, using blanket stitch (see box). Leave a small hole at the very top.

### You will need:

- felt in two different colours
- pins and an embroidery needle
- embroidery thread
- ribbon

### TOP TIP

This is also a great way to protect a memory stick!

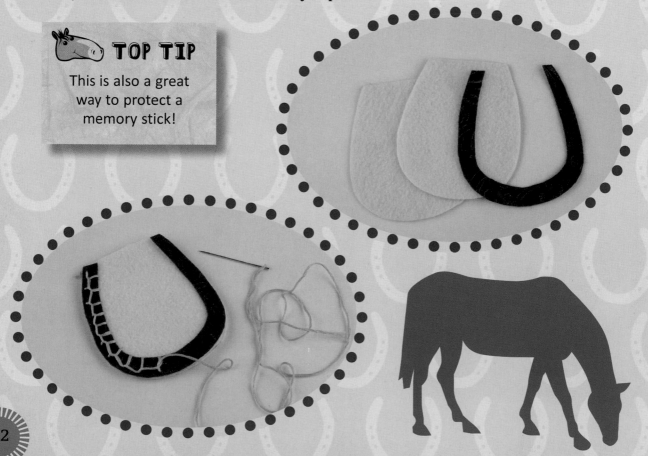

**3** Thread your key on to the ribbon, and pass both ends into the horseshoe and through the hole at the top. Trim the ribbon until you are happy that the pendant sits in the right place.

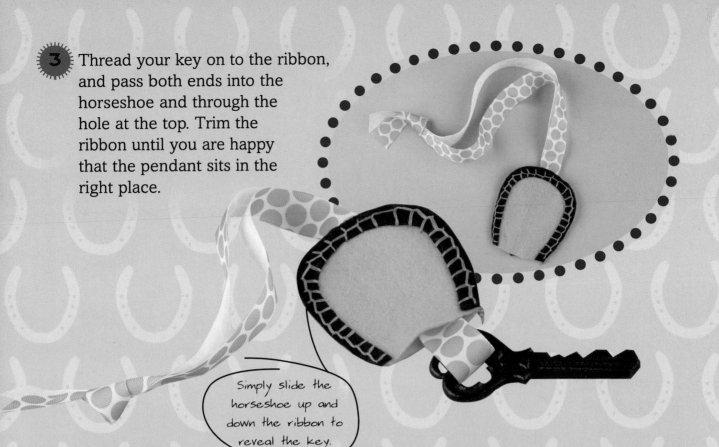

Simply slide the horseshoe up and down the ribbon to reveal the key.

## Stitching skills

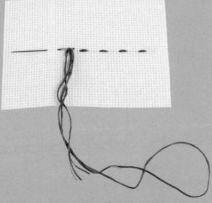

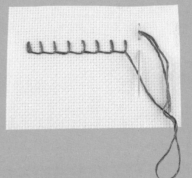

### Blanket stitch

Knot the thread and push the needle up through the fabric. Push the needle back into the fabric right next to the stitch and back up directly below it, catching the loose end to make a loop. Carry on pushing the needle down and up through the fabric, catching a loop each time.

### Running stitch

The simplest stitch. Knot the thread, and push the needle up through the fabric. Push it down and back up through the fabric to make a dotted line.

# Pretty pony notice board

This padded notice board is the perfect place to display certificates and rosettes.

## You will need:

- cheap art canvas with a wooden frame
- wadding (or layers of packing foam)
- drawing pins or a staple gun
- fabric with a horse print, 20 cm (8 in.) longer and wider than your canvas
- lengths of ribbon
- paper fasteners

**1** Stretch several layers of wadding or packing foam over the canvas. Secure it to the back of the frame using drawing pins, or ask an adult to help you use a staple gun.

**2** Cover your frame with fabric, and pin or staple it to the frame one edge at a time, folding the corners as if you were wrapping a present.

**3** Drape lengths of ribbon across the frame in a diagonal pattern, securing them to the back of the frame in the same way.

**4** Keep the ribbons in place by making holes at each point where two ribbons cross, and pushing a paper fastener through to hold the ribbons to the canvas. Ask an adult to help you with this step, and remember to protect the surface you are working on.

If you already have a cork notice board, this is a good way to customize it! Hold the ribbons in place using drawing pins instead of paper fasteners.

# 5 projects... for using fabric

Let your imagination take the reins, and add a touch of horse magic to fabric.

- Turn one of the templates (see page 31) into a foam stamp, dip it into fabric paint, and print a sheet of cotton with a horsey design.

- Decorate a lampshade with horsey designs.

- Edge a horse blanket with blanket stitch (see page 13), and embroider your initials using running stitch.

- Choose one of the templates and embroider it on to a T-shirt, dress or skirt.

- Wrap leftover wadding and fabric around a clothes hanger to make a padded hanger. It's the perfect way to store riding gear or other special clothes.

# Get crafty with me.

Horses are adorable! Spread the word, with this pretty, personalized stationery.

## Horse notebook and cards

Download the templates (see page 31) to make this notebook and matching horsey stationery.

**1** Cut out three identical squares of cardboard from the box, and glue them together to make a base for your stamp. Leave to dry overnight.

**2** Print and cut out your chosen template, and glue it to a piece of craft foam. Cut around the shape again, so you have a foam shape.

**3** Glue the foam shape on to the cardboard base. Your stamp is ready to use.

### You will need:

- corrugated cardboard
- craft foam
- scissors
- PVA glue
- ink pad
- plain notebook
- notepaper and envelopes

### Pretty postcards

Print one of the horse silhouettes (see page 31 for the website link) and transfer it on to patterned paper – origami paper is perfect. Cut out the shapes and glue on to blank postcards. Glue on sequins or beads for eyes.

**4** Press the stamp on to an ink pad (or carefully brush on a very thin layer of paint) and stamp across the cover of your notebook and once on each sheet of notepaper and envelope.

## Pet view

If you are lucky enough to ride a horse, why not turn your decorated notebook into an equestrian record book.

Decorate a notebook by printing a repeated pattern with your stamp.

# Galloping horses

There are loads of ways to use these gorgeous galloping horses. Frame them to make 3D art, jazz up greetings cards, or make a whole herd to gallop across your bedroom wall!

**1** Follow the weblink on page 31, find and print the galloping horses template and transfer it on to card. You will need one body, two back legs and two front legs for each horse. Use a pin to make a hole through the centre of each cross on the horse's legs and body.

**2** Cut out the pieces, and decorate with pens, paints or patterned paper. You could add a mane or bridle using embroidery thread or wool.

**3** Use paper fasteners to attach the legs to the body in pairs.

## You will need:

- A5 sheet of medium white card
- patterned paper
- colouring pens or paints
- pin
- paper fasteners
- embroidery thread or wool

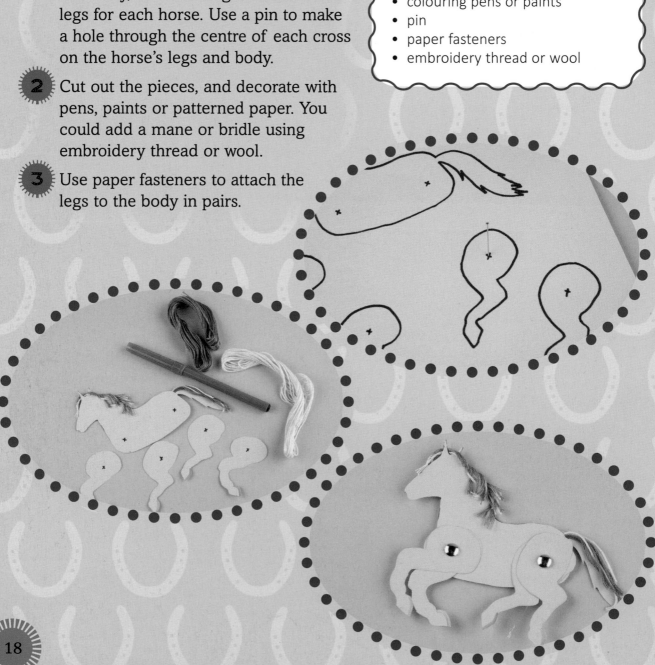

# 5 ways... to paint different coats

- Brush watery grey paint over the horse, and sprinkle on salt. When the paint is dry, brush the salt off for a dappled coat.

- Use acrylic paint to make a shiny chestnut coat.

- Block out patches with white wax crayon, then paint over the top to create an Appaloosa or piebald effect.

- Flick paint on with a toothbrush for a roan coat.

- Cover the body in watery brown paint, and dab black paint on the legs and back for a bay coat.

Will your horse trot, canter or gallop?

# Ho,  e-  o,.e DIY project

You might not be able to bring horses home with you, but you can fill your bedroom with reminders of your BFFs - best fetlocked friends!

## Pony pottery

Head to a pottery-painting studio to make this galloping horse plate. If you don't have a studio near you, use the steps to customize paper plates or a clock face instead.

### At home

Choose a silhouette design from page 31 and transfer it on to low-tack sticky labels. You will need 30 copies. Carefully cut them out and bring them with you to the pottery studio.

### At the studio

Choose the plate, bowl or mug you would like to decorate. Pick your paint – you will need to use three different shades of the same colour.

1. Start by sticking ten stickers on to the plate, leaving lots of space between them. Sponge or paint the lightest shade all over the plate.

2. When the paint is dry to the touch, stick another ten stickers on to the plate. Space them out randomly, overlapping the existing stickers if you like. Sponge over the next lightest shade of paint.

3. When this layer of paint is dry to the touch, add the last ten stickers and sponge or paint over the darkest shade.

## You will need:

- sheet of reusable, easy-peel stickers or labels
- pencil, scissors, tracing paper
- unglazed plate, bowl or mug to decorate

**4** Once this final layer is dry, carefully peel off all the stickers, to reveal your horses, horseshoes or other shapes in three different colours. The plate can now be glazed and fired by the studio.

Painted pottery has to be glazed and fired before you can use it, but you could use this method to decorate paper plates or other objects for display.

## DIY rosette

Pretty paper rosettes will add pony club chic to your bedroom. Pleat a sheet of pretty A5 paper by folding the short end under and over, like an accordion. The pleats should be around 2 cm (¾ in.) wide. Fold the pleated strip in half, and stick the facing sides together with double-sided tape. Open the paper up like a fan. Repeat with a second and third sheet of paper. Tape the three shapes together to make a rosette. Tape on two tails, and stick on a button for the centre disc.

You could hang your rosettes on strings, or stick clusters of them to walls and furniture.

### Pet view

Rosettes have been used to decorate horses' bridles for hundreds of years. They are traditionally made from ribbon pleated to look like a flower.

# Get arty

Horses have always inspired artists. Now it's your turn! Learn how to photograph these beautiful creatures and make a frame to show off your best shots.

## At the stable door

This super-cute frame is the perfect way to display photographs or drawings of your horse.

1. Cut two pieces of A5 corrugated cardboard. Carefully pull the front layer of paper off piece A, to reveal the ridges below.

2. Cut piece B in half. Stick one of the halves on to piece A, with the ridges facing out. Stick your photograph on to the top half of piece A.

3. Using the template on the website (see page 31), cut two hinge-shaped pieces of fabric. Use them to join the top half of piece B to piece A, so that it can open and close.

### You will need:

- corrugated cardboard (use an old box)
- scrap of fabric
- PVA glue, scissors, ruler, pencil
- favourite horse photograph
- decorations to customize your design

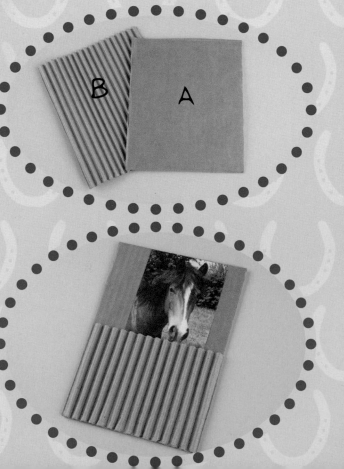

### Pet view

Remember, I may be scared of your camera. Keep your distance and turn off the flash and sound effects.

## 5 tips... for taking great photographs

- Choose a natural background, such as trees or fields.

- Stand at a distance and keep your camera level with the horse's shoulders. Use your camera to zoom in when you want to take close-ups.

- Set your camera to take action shots, even if the horse is standing still. A horse's ears and tail are always on the move.

- If you are photographing a horse and a person together, snap them when they are looking at each other, instead of the camera.

- Try to capture pictures of the horse with its ears forwards. You can encourage a horse to prick up its ears by making a soft whistling sound.

4 You can make a stand for your frame by downloading the template, cutting the shape out of card and gluing it to the back of your frame.

Add decorations, such as horseshoes and a name plaque, to make your pony look at home.

# Horsehair jewellery

Did you know that hair collected from horses is used to make violin bows and make-up brushes? It can even be woven into fabric and jewellery, like this beautiful bracelet.

## You will need:

- 15 to 30 long strands of horse hair, collected from a pulling comb or clipped with permission from the owner
- sticky tape
- superglue
- bracelet clasp from a bead shop

 **TOP TIP**

Work on a surface that won't be damaged, such as newspaper.

**1** Gather the hairs together and tie a knot at one end. Tape the knot to a flat surface to hold it in place while you work.

**2** Split the bundle of hairs into three equal strands. Plait the strands tightly, stopping when the braid is long enough to circle your wrist. Tie a second knot.

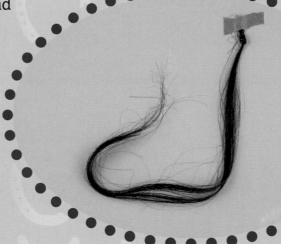

**3** Ask an adult to help you dab superglue on each end of the braid, just in front of the knots. When the glue has dried, cut the knots off and the glue will hold the braid in place.

**4** Push each end of the braid into the bracelet clasps. Ask an adult to help you clamp them in place.

A gorgeous gift for a horse-loving friend.

### Pet view

Horses naturally shed hair from their manes and tails, and they can also be clipped or "pulled" as part of grooming.

# Throw a pony party!

Celebrate how much you love horses by throwing a party to remember your favourite horse's birthday.

## Pony tail bunting

This tassel bunting is perfect for a pony party – create a multicoloured parade of pony tails.

### You will need:

- tissue paper (or old plastic carrier bags, fabric or newspaper)
- long length of colourful string or wool
- scissors

1. To make each tassel, fold a sheet of tissue paper in half lengthways and then widthways, to make a rectangle.

2. Starting from the unfolded end, make long cuts in the paper about 2 cm (¾ in.) apart, cutting towards the fold. Stop cutting 4 cm (1½ in.) from the fold.

**3** Unfold the paper once, then roll it into a sausage shape from long edge to long edge.

**4** Twist the middle section of the sausage, loop it over the string then twist it again to hold the tassel in place.

Keep adding tassels until you run out of string, or the party starts!

# Rosette cupcakes

These cute cupcakes will be a winner for any horse lover. Make them to celebrate birthdays, special occasions or equestrian events.

**1** Using a rolling pin dusted with icing sugar, roll out the yellow icing until it is around 3 mm thick. Use the scone cutter to cut 12 circles with frilled edges.

**2** Roll out the blue icing and cut 12 circles with the small round cutter. With the leftover blue icing, cut 24 short rectangles, removing a triangle-shaped piece from each end.

**3** Assemble each rosette using dabs of wet glacé icing to stick. Layer two blue ribbons first, followed by a yellow frilled circle and a smaller blue circle.

**4** Add decorations to the centre of each rosette.

## You will need:

- 12 undecorated cupcakes
- ready-to-roll fondant icing in yellow and blue (or any two colours of your choosing)
- rolling pin
- scone cutter with frilled edge
- round cookie cutter, slightly smaller than the scone cutter
- butter or table knife
- glacé icing (1 tbsp. of icing sugar mixed with enough water to make a thick paste)
- edible decorations

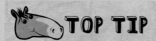

## TOP TIP

If you can't get hold of scone and cookie cutters, use the templates on the website (see page 31).

# 5 great ideas... for gifts and favours

These projects make great gifts or party favours for horse-mad guests.

- Add initials to the centre of paper rosettes (see page 21) to make place settings.

- Make pretty horse postcards as invitations (see page 16).

- Organize a pottery-painting party using the tips on page 20 – just have a huge pile of stickers and templates ready to go.

- Make personalized decorated horseshoes for your guests to hang up at home (see page 8).

- Cover cheap picture frames or pencil pots with horsey découpage for a gift so stylish, no one will guess how simple it was to make!

# Horse facts

## 5 facts... for horse lovers

- Around 400,000 horses and ponies live in the UK.

- In Mongolia in 2013, more than 11,000 horses took part in the world's largest horse parade.

- Horses' hooves grow around 6 mm ($\frac{1}{4}$ in.) every month – that's twice as fast as your fingernails, so it's important that horses see a farrier regularly.

- Horses have the largest eyes of any land animal, except ostriches. Because their eyes are on the sides of their heads, horses can see in almost every direction at once.

- Scientists at Southampton University recently discovered that horses' favourite flavours are fenugreek, banana and cherry!

## Find out more

Pony Club UK is a great website for young people interested in riding and looking after horses.
**www.pcuk.org**

The British Horse Society has lots of information about where and how to ride horses.
**www.bhs.org.uk**

Find out where to watch horses and ponies in action at the British Equestrian Federation website.
**www.bef.co.uk**

# Templates

Visit **www.raintree.co.uk/content/download** and select "Handy Horse Projects" to download free templates to use with the projects in this book. You can also use them to create your own horse designs. Once you have printed a template, follow these tips to transfer it to the material you are working with.

- Use masking tape to hold a sheet of tracing or baking paper over your chosen design and draw over the outline with a soft pencil.

- Tape the paper on to the surface you'd like to transfer the picture to.

- Draw over the lines using a pen with a hard point.

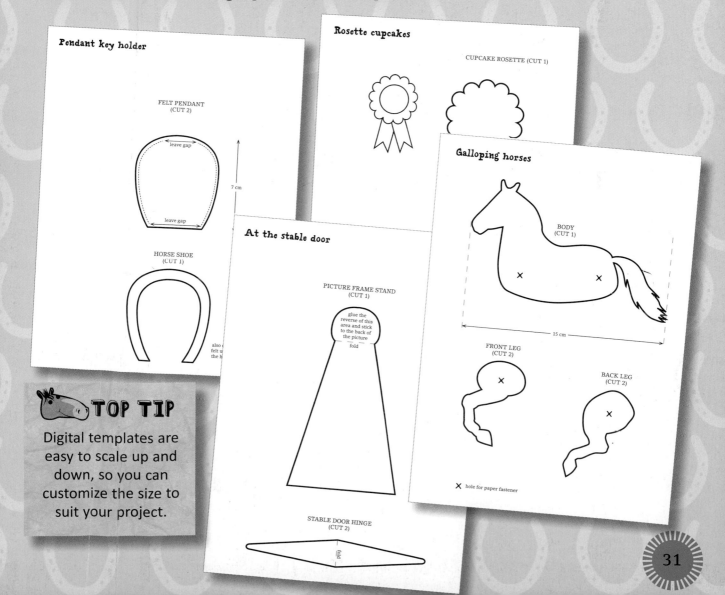

**Pendant key holder**

FELT PENDANT
(CUT 2)

leave gap

leave gap

7 cm

HORSE SHOE
(CUT 1)

**Rosette cupcakes**

CUPCAKE ROSETTE (CUT 1)

**Galloping horses**

BODY
(CUT 1)

15 cm

FRONT LEG
(CUT 2)

BACK LEG
(CUT 2)

✗ hole for paper fastener

**At the stable door**

PICTURE FRAME STAND
(CUT 1)

glue the reverse of this area and stick to the back of the picture

fold

STABLE DOOR HINGE
(CUT 2)

fold

**TOP TIP**

Digital templates are easy to scale up and down, so you can customize the size to suit your project.

# Index